TODAY IS
CASH

Spend It Wisely, Invest It Purposefully
Cherish It Dearly

BY
Peggy McColl
New York Times Best Selling Author
With Co-Author Ava

Hasmark
PUBLISHING
INTERNATIONAL

ISBN 13: 978-1-77482-243-2
ISBN 10: 1774822431

Published by:

Hasmark Publishing International

Layout Artist: Amit Dey amit@hasmarkpublishing.com

IMPORTANT DISCLAIMERS

The author has done their best to present accurate and up-to-date information in this book but cannot guarantee that the information is correct or will suit your particular situation. Further, the publisher has used its best efforts in preparing this book, and the information provided herein is provided "as is."

We can't guarantee any results from the use of our programs or any of the information contained in this book, though we genuinely believe that this information will help you reach your goals. Like with any program, your results are limited by your willingness to take action as well as factors outside of your control and our control. By reading this book and enrolling in any programs you hereby understand the potential risks when embarking upon a goal achievement journey of any kind and are fully aware and take responsibility for your own results holding Peggy McColl and Dynamic Destinies Inc. harmless.

This is intended for informational purposes only and should not be used as the primary basis for an investment decision.

Consult a financial advisor for your personal situation. Please consider the investment objectives, risks, fees, and expenses carefully before investing in anything. Past performance does not guarantee future results.

For more disclaimers that may apply, please view the most up to date information on:

http://peggymccoll.com

Cover design by Killer Covers **Book layout** by Hasmark Publishing **Editing** by Kathryn Young First Edition, 2023

DEDICATION

This book is dedicated to my precious granddaughter, Aria, and my incredible grandson, James.

Spending time with both of you is a cherished treasure that fills my heart with joy and gratitude. Your presence and the moments we share together are the most valuable investments in my life. May this book inspire you to embrace the currency of time and make each day count.

TABLE OF CONTENTS

AN EXTRAORDINARY JOURNEY

Dear Reader,

Welcome to a journey that is not measured in miles or kilometers but in moments, hours, and days. A journey that is both a tale and a guide, a narrative, and a compass. This is a book that straddles the realms of fiction and non-fiction, threading together a story that carries a profound truth and a guide that imparts practical wisdom. Welcome to *Today is Cash*.

The concept of *Today is Cash* came to me during a time of great personal upheaval. I was diagnosed with metastatic cancer, a term that takes your breath away and turns your world upside down in an instant. In the throes of this confrontation with mortality, I had a revelation about the fleeting and precious nature of time. *Time, I realized, is the most valuable currency we own, and how we choose to spend it can define the richness of our lives.*

The inherent value of each moment, each breath, and each heartbeat became painfully clear. The diagnosis jolted me from the ordinary rhythms of life into a reality where time was no longer a given, but a gift—a precious, fragile gift that needed to be cherished, not squandered.

The words "Today is Cash" held profound significance for me. They became my mantra, a daily reminder of the importance of investing my time wisely. I soon realized that this concept held universal truth, a wisdom that could benefit everyone, regardless of their age or circumstance.

That's how this unique book was born. It's a blend of storytelling and practical guidance, designed to captivate your imagination while also equipping you with the tools to make meaningful changes in your own life.

In the **Narrative** chapters, you'll meet a gentleman who, much like me, discovers the transformational power of viewing time as a precious commodity. His journey echoes the sentiments I felt upon my own revelation, and I hope his story resonates with you.

But this book is more than just a tale—it's a map, a guide to understanding and implementing the Today is Cash philosophy into your own life. It's an invitation to pause and reflect, to consider how you're spending your moments, your hours, and your days. Importantly, it also provides practical strategies for managing your time and maximizing its value, helping you to live a more fulfilling, balanced, and intentional life.

As you read, study, and apply what's written in the **Compass** chapters, remember that every day is a deposit, a sum of time given to you to spend. But unlike money, time cannot be earned back once it's spent. It is, indeed, your most valuable asset. Use it wisely. Invest it purposefully. Cherish it dearly.

My hope is that *Today is Cash* will inspire you to see the value in each moment, to seize the day, and to live your life to its fullest potential. After all, our lives are made up of moments. Let's make each one count.

Welcome to the journey. Let's begin.

THE
NARRATIVE

CHAPTER 1

A NEW JOURNEY

In the half-light of dawn, the city snored under the sheets of sleep, oblivious of the new day inching in. One by one, buildings began to glow, their pale, artificial lights struggling to match the brightness of the waking sun. And in the middle of this grand urban theater, there sat a man by a window, his silhouetted form caressed by the first rays of the sunrise.

His name is Mitch Lincoln, a wealthy man many considered an enigma, a living paradox. Mitch is not one for the promise of the morrow or the poetry of yesteryears. No, he is the herald of the present, a purveyor of the most precious commodity of our time—the tangible, volatile, and unpredictable *today*. "Today is Cash," Mitch would say, his eyes sparkling with a mystery few could unravel.

He sat in his favorite chair by the window, meditating on one powerful idea, reiterating his mantra, "Today is Cash," as he quietly became one with this truth.

The world had yet to stir, the city's heartbeat was just beginning its rhythm, and Mitch Lincoln was ready for the day. His gaze steady on the horizon, he watched the golden orb of the sun ascend, marking the start of another growth day, another page in his unending ledger. And with a quiet resolve, he uttered his mantra once more, "Today is Cash."

As these words floated in the morning air, a gentle breeze seemed to carry them across the cityscape. The day was just beginning, and so was Mitch's chase, where time was the game, and every passing moment was a coin dropped in the fountain of the relentless present.

And thus, Mitch's story unfolds, a tale of a man whose life was the embodiment of a profound paradox, where the ticking clock was not an enemy but a partner, and where every dawn brought not just a new day, but a fresh stack of bills to be earned, circulated, and cherished. You see, Mitch understood the value of investments. Mitch understood how to earn money.

So, fasten your seatbelt, dear reader, for the clock is ticking and Mitch Lincoln waits for no one. Dive into his world, where every heartbeat is a currency, and every moment has its price. After all, Today is Cash.

CHAPTER 2

THE CHASE BEGINS

Today was his birthday. He was thirty-nine years old, yet he had no special plans, no special someone to share his day with. As Mitch leaned back in his chair, his gaze still locked on the four screens in front of him, he found himself reminiscing about his journey thus far. He was a man at the pinnacle of the world, and he knew with certainty, his quest for prosperity had been well worth the investment of time and energy. While deep in thought, his fingers drummed rhythmically on the polished mahogany of his desk, each tap echoing the ticking of the antique French wall clock behind him. So why did he feel unsettled, as if he were missing out on something just beyond his reach?

For Mitch, every day started with numbers—numbers that danced on the digital screens of his multiple monitors, a symphony of the world's economies in real-time. His fingers flew across the keyboard, his eyes narrowing at the fluctuating digits on the screens. Yet, he didn't seek wealth in the mere accumulation of these figures. His pursuit was far more profound.

"Today is Cash," he repeated to himself. Today held the secret to his true wealth, a wealth that was more than just figures in a bank account. Mitch understood that how he invested his time today would determine how he spent his tomorrows.

His mind traveled back to his humble beginnings, to a time when he was overwhelmed in debt, when he had nothing but a dream. He remembered the day that he first understood the true value of *today*. He was a paperboy back then, and the one phrase his manager always told him was, "Today's news is tomorrow's trash."

The words had lodged in his young mind, their meaning only becoming clear as he ascended in life. *The power of today was passing, yet potent. The value of today diminished by tomorrow, just as today's news became tomorrow's trash.*

A soft chime interrupted his thoughts, pulling him back to the present. A new email had arrived. Mitch leaned forward to read it. It was an invitation from the Young Entrepreneurs Association, an opportunity to address a crowd of young entrepreneurs at their annual awards banquet. He smiled. He didn't accept many speaking engagements, but this was intriguing. This was a chance to give back, to guide the new generation, to share his secret of *today*. He replied to the association president and accepted the invitation.

Mitch got up from his chair, restless with thoughts and ideas for the speech, and moved towards the window. The city was wide awake now, buzzing with life, everyone engrossed in their personal chase of time. As he looked at the city, a profound realization suddenly washed over him as if the universe had decided he was ready to understand. *True wealth was not just in accumulating riches, but in shaping the world, impacting lives, and leaving a legacy.*

Mitch laughed with surprise at his insight. Perhaps this was the something he had been elusively yearning for. His mantra, "Today is Cash," now had a new dimension. Each day was not just about making money, but about making a difference.

His heart pounded in his chest, as he thought about giving back, and he realized he was filled with a new purpose. Today, Mitch Lincoln would embark on a new chapter of his life. He had uncovered the secret to true prosperity— the balance of wealth and wisdom—and now he wanted to share it with the world.

CHAPTER 3

THE SPEECH

Mitch's sleek black Jaguar purred through the bustling city, weaving between high-rises that seemed to scrape the skies. His destination was the grand auditorium at the Barclay Hotel. This is where Mitch Lincoln, a beacon of knowledge, was due to share his wisdom. Stopped at a light, his fingers tapped restlessly on the steering wheel, a testament to the pulsing anticipation coursing through him. He wasn't nervous; he had long since conquered fear. He was simply eager, ready to make a difference.

Leaving his Jag with an efficient young valet, he entered the hotel and quickly found the auditorium. The association president greeted him with a big smile and then guided him backstage. After the president's lengthy introduction that highlighted his many financial accomplishments, it was time.

Stepping onto the stage under the warm, glowing lights, Mitch looked out into the sea of eager faces, the next generation of entrepreneurs, dreamers, and go-getters. For a moment, he saw his younger self in their wide, hopeful eyes. This was his opportunity and his responsibility.

With a gentle clearing of his throat, he began, "They say time is money. But that's not entirely true. Time is more than money; it's *life*. Today, right now, this very moment, is your life." A hush fell over the crowd. All eyes were locked onto Mitch. This was probably not what they had expected from a multimillionaire known for making money.

Mitch had a unique way of captivating a crowd. He was a gifted storyteller. As he moved purposefully across the stage all eyes followed him and took in every word.

"The world would have you believe that wealth is measured in dollars and cents. But wealth, my friends, is measured in *moments*. Every day is a treasure trove of opportunities and experiences. My mantra is "Today is Cash," but that doesn't just mean making money today. It means investing time wisely making memories, forging connections, living to the fullest."

He paused, letting his words wash over the young minds. He could see the change in their eyes; curiosity had replaced their initial uncertainty.

"True prosperity lies in finding the balance. Yes, financial stability is crucial. But so is personal growth, so are relationships, so is your happiness. Don't just work to *earn*, work to *learn*. Don't just make connections to *profit*, make connections to *impact*. The secret to true wealth is not to exploit today but to embrace it and cherish every precious moment."

As his words echoed in the silent auditorium, a wave of realization swept through the audience. Heads were nodding. This was not just a speech; it was a life lesson, a guide to true prosperity. And for Mitch, this was not just another day, another speech; it was the first step in making a difference. Today, he didn't just add numbers to his account; he added value to lives.

After the speech and the audience's enthusiastic applause, as a special gift to all in attendance, Mitch gave out silicon bracelets embossed with the words "Today is Cash" as a reminder of the life-changing message he had shared.

Off the stage now, a sense of contentment washed over Mitch as the young entrepreneurs hurried forward to shake his hand. He knew his journey to give back was just beginning. He would approach life each day with a new mind, a mind open for positive change. Thankfully he had taken the first step, and that was what mattered. Today is Cash, and today, he had struck gold.

CHAPTER 4

A NEW DIRECTION

The sun had long since set when Mitch returned to his office. His mind was still filled with the echoes of applause, the faces of the young crowd, their rapt attention, and the final roaring standing ovation. His speech had ignited something within them, and in return, their eagerness had kindled a spark within him. His journey to true prosperity and giving back had taken on a new, more meaningful impression.

In the quiet solitude of his office, Mitch found himself looking at his life in a new light. What were once just financial achievements and compounded growth now felt like a reward for the investment he made each day. His impact today had gone beyond just words. It was a step towards change, towards shaping a better future. And that, he realized, was his real wealth.

The computer screens that once flashed market trends and numbers now stood dark and silent. Mitch couldn't help but smile. His view of success was shifting, from the blinding glare of wealth to the softer glow of impact. "Today is cash," he murmured, his mind swimming in the depth of those words.

He switched on his computer and began to draft an email. His contacts were vast, a network of influential individuals and corporations. Today, he would leverage those connections, not for profits but for a greater cause. He typed out his new plan, his vision for a program that would continue his great work to fund and mentor start-ups and young entrepreneurs. He would share his wisdom, his experience, and his resources to help others prosper and invite other successful entrepreneurs to join him.

He hit the send button, feeling a sense of accomplishment wash over him. Today, he had not just earned or spent, but invested—invested in the future, in dreams, in lives. His mantra was taking on a life of its own, moving beyond him, beyond his story.

As Mitch looked out over the city one last time before calling it a day, his heart swelled with anticipation. He was on a new path, a path of true wealth and prosperity, where every day held the promise of impact, and every moment was an opportunity to make a difference. Because Today is Cash, he was ready to spend it wisely.

CHAPTER 5

THE RIPPLE EFFECT

Weeks slipped by since Mitch's email was sent, but its positive ripples were immediate and still being felt as many chose to join him on this quest. His initiative, aptly named Today is Cash, had become a beacon for young entrepreneurs, and along with his new business partners, the launch was spreading faster than a virus. From all corners of the world, applications from young and new entrepreneurs poured in, each one brimming with ideas ready to reshape the future.

Mitch's office had transformed. Gone were the strict financial graphs and numbers that once dominated his screens. Now, innovative ideas and fresh perspectives from enthusiastic start-ups took center stage. Each day, Mitch immersed himself in these vibrant plans, relishing in the pulse of innovation. He was in his glory.

His wealth was growing, but not just in his bank account. He was accumulating a wealth of ideas, relationships, and impact. The worldwide difference-making he sought was manifesting. Yet, Mitch knew there was more to be done, more lives to touch, more dreams to foster.

One day, amidst the pile of applications, one particular proposal caught his eye. It was a project for sustainable energy, helmed by a young engineer named Kayla Green. Her passion resonated in her words; her determination reflected in her plan. Mitch was captivated. Here was a dream that held the promise to change the world. He picked up his phone and dialed a number, setting in motion a chain of events that would change not just Kayla's life, but his own as well. Little did Mitch know, but Kayla was going to have an even greater impression on his life, as she would ultimately become his wife.

As Mitch guided Kayla and her team, he found himself a student again. Every discussion, every meeting was a lesson in resilience, innovation, and passion. He was not just an investor and mentor but also a mentee, learning about the world from fresh, youthful perspectives.

The Today is Cash initiative was transforming millions of lives in significantly positive ways, and Mitch was at the heart of it. Every day, he was not just investing his money but also his time, his knowledge. He was building a legacy, one start-up at a time, each a testament to his belief that "Today is Cash."

Mitch ended each day with a sense of contentment, a sense of fulfillment. He was wealthy, but not just with money. He was rich in experience, in relationships, in satisfaction. He was prosperous, but his prosperity was now measured in his impact, his legacy. Mitch Lincoln had discovered the secret to true wealth and was sharing it with the world, one day at a time.

CHAPTER 6

THE ECHO OF SUCCESS

Months turned into a year since Mitch had launched his Today is Cash initiative. He and Kayla were blissfully married now and supportive of each other's dreams and goals. Mitch's program had birthed countless successful projects, each a beacon of innovation and progress. Yet, for Mitch, the most significant measure of success was not in the number of start-ups or the profits they turned. It was in the lives he had touched, the dreams he had helped realize, including his own of meeting the woman of his dreams.

Among the thriving ventures was Kayla's sustainable energy project. It had become a resounding success, contributing significantly to the city's power grid, and sparking a revolution in renewable energy sources. As Mitch stood next to Kayla at the inauguration ceremony of her project's expansion, he could not help but feel a deep sense of pride. Here was an idea she birthed but he had nurtured, a dream he had believed in, now a reality impacting the city, the world. This was another example of true wealth and prosperity.

News of Mitch's journey to true prosperity had spread far and wide. He was no longer just Mitch Lincoln, the multimillionaire. He was Mitch Lincoln, the visionary, the mentor, the changemaker. His story was no longer about his rise to wealth. It was about his journey to impact, his pursuit of balance, his belief in today.

Yet, Mitch was far from done. His mantra, "Today is Cash," still echoed in his mind, a constant reminder that every new day was a fresh opportunity. He continued to nurture new projects, continued to share his wisdom with eager entrepreneurs. He had discovered that the secret to true prosperity was not a destination but a journey, a constant pursuit of balance and impact.

As the sun set on another fulfilling day, Mitch sat in his home office, his gaze out at the city he had helped shape. He was no longer just a spectator to the twinkling lights; he was a part of them, a part of their stories, their dreams. His journey had brought him wealth, wisdom, and a profound understanding of his mantra. Today was indeed cash, a currency to be spent not just on *gaining* but also on *giving*. This resulted in the highest feeling of life fulfillment.

Mitch leaned back in his chair, a soft smile playing on his lips. He had come a long way, from a man chasing the present to a man shaping the future. Mitch decided to join Kayla, who had already retired for the night. As he put his head on the pillow, he reflected on the understanding that with each sunrise, a new day awaited, brimming with possibilities, promising opportunities to make a difference.

He fell asleep with his mantra playing softly in his mind and looking forward to how he would invest his tomorrow.

CHAPTER 7

TOMORROW'S TODAY

As the dawn of a new day spread across the cityscape, Mitch found himself at a familiar window, gazing at an all too familiar view ready to do his morning meditation. Yet, everything felt different. The city was no longer just a mechanical entity. It had a pulse, a heart that beat with the hopes and dreams of the people Mitch had touched, the ventures he had fostered.

Mitch's day always began with a joyous expectancy. Reviewing his emails, he was touched with stories, stories of dreams being nurtured and ideas for lives being impacted by his Today is Cash initiative. A flood of emails awaited his attention, each one a testament to the changes his journey had sparked.

One email stood out among the rest. It was from a renowned university, inviting Mitch to receive an honorary doctorate for his contributions to the entrepreneurial world. A surge of pride welled up within him. Recognition was not his goal, but it was gratifying to see his efforts being acknowledged on such a grand scale.

However, Mitch saw in this invitation more than just an accolade. He saw an opportunity to reach a wider audience, to inspire more young minds, to further echo his philosophy of Today is Cash. This was not just an acknowledgment; it was a platform, a chance to amplify his impact.

Accepting the invitation, Mitch found himself standing in yet another grand auditorium of the university a few weeks later, adorned in the traditional cap and gown. His heart pounded with anticipation as he looked out into the sea of eager faces. These were the innovators of tomorrow, the dreamers waiting to make their mark on the world. Kayla joined him for this momentous occasion. She sat on the first row, her pride in him radiating on her beautiful face.

With a firm grip on the lectern, Mitch began, "Time, my friends, is the great equalizer. It does not discriminate. We all have the same twenty-four hours. But what differentiates us is how we use those hours. The secret to true wealth and prosperity lies not in the *tomorrows* or *yesterdays*, but in the *todays*. Each moment of today is precious. Each second represents currency to be spent wisely."

His words echoed in the hall, each thought and idea resonating with the rapt audience. Today, Mitch was not just receiving an honor. He was furthering his journey of true prosperity, making a difference, leaving a legacy. He was shaping the innovators of tomorrow by guiding them today.

As he concluded his speech, a wave of applause swept across the hall. Each clap was a testament to his impact, each cheer an affirmation of his journey. Today, Mitch had not just received an honor, he had sown the seeds of his Today is Cash philosophy in fresh minds, setting the stage for a new generation of dreamers and doers.

Tomorrow was an unknown entity, but Mitch was certain of one thing—his journey of impacting lives, of true prosperity, would continue because he was completely committed. After all, every tomorrow would become a today, and for Mitch Lincoln, and for all those he had taught his philosophy, Today is Cash.

CHAPTER 8

THE LEGACY

Eight years had passed since Mitch had embarked on his journey of true prosperity. His Today is Cash initiative had transcended borders, reaching out to entrepreneurs across the world. His philosophy had been sown in the minds of the young, fostering a new generation of balanced prosperity-seekers.

But for Mitch, it was more than just a global movement. It was his legacy.

As the sun dipped below the horizon, painting the sky in hues of gold and crimson, Mitch sat in his preferred chair reviewing several new proposals, appreciating that his office was now a hub for innovation and mentorship. His gaze fell on the wall filled with photographs, each one a story of dreams realized, and lives changed. This was his wealth. This was his prosperity.

Among the smiling faces, he found Kayla's, her project now a global entity pushing boundaries in sustainable energy. His heart swelled with pride. This was not just her success; it was his too. He had not just invested in her project; he had believed in her dream. And today, her dream was illuminating the world.

Mitch's life had come full circle. He was no longer chasing the future, no longer anchored to the past. He was living in the now, in the today. Each day was an opportunity, a currency that he spent wisely. He had indeed discovered the secret to true wealth and prosperity, but it was no longer a secret. He had shared it with the world, and the world had embraced it.

Retiring to their home later that night, Mitch felt a contentment that was comforting. He had money, but his real wealth lay in the lives he had touched, the changes he had ignited, and the legacy he was leaving behind. His journey was far from over, but he had made peace with the road ahead. Because he knew that no matter what tomorrow held, it would eventually become today, and Today is Cash.

Mitch closed his eyes, his heart echoing his mantra. He had started his journey as a man of wealth. Now, he was a man of value with a beautiful wife and two children by his side. His legacy was not his fortune; it was his philosophy, his belief in the importance of today.

The world knew him as Mitch Lincoln, the multimillionaire entrepreneur turned mentor. But for Mitch, he was simply a man who understood the value of today. Today, he had not just lived; he had made a difference. Today, he had not just earned; he had learned, given, and grown.

Today, Mitch had made his cash count.

THE COMPASS

YOUR JOURNEY FORWARD

Dear Reader,

I am writing this on the cusp of my 65th birthday and grateful to be in remission from cancer. I've lived through six and a half decades, countless moments and experiences, and I find myself looking back in awe of the speed at which it all went by. Time truly is fleeting. It runs like water through our fingers, and the tighter we try to hold it, the faster it seems to slip away.

That's why I wrote this book. My experience with cancer wasn't just a wake-up call about my health. It was a wake-up call about how I was spending, or rather, investing my time. Each moment that we are given on this earth is a precious commodity, an irreplaceable asset.

Let me tell you a story. When my mother was diagnosed with terminal cancer, she was given six months to live. She knew how precious her time was and when her end would come. She was at peace. The family gently asked her what she would like to do during these months. Would she like to travel? Would she like to have unique experiences that she had only dreamed of? But she didn't want to travel or go anywhere—she said she only wanted to be with family and friends as that is what felt joyful and fulfilling to her. Every day became a gift that she chose to spend wisely.

In the pages that follow, you'll find tools and strategies to help you understand, manage, and value your time in ways you may not have considered before. But more than that, you'll hopefully find a new perspective on life.

Time is a currency that we all have, rich or poor, young, or old. It's the great equalizer, but it's also the one asset that we can never earn more of. Once spent, it's gone forever. But, if invested wisely, it can yield infinite returns in happiness, fulfilment, and peace.

As you journey through these chapters, my hope is that you don't just read the words, but truly absorb their meaning. Allow them to change the way you think about time, about life. The aim isn't to create a whirlwind of productivity or a relentless chase of accomplishments. Instead, it's about understanding the value of each moment and making conscious choices about how you spend your time.

We are all given an unknown amount of time in this life. I was reminded of that in a profound and terrifying way.

But every day, every moment, holds the promise of something beautiful. It's up to us to see that promise and make the most of it.

Remember, Today is Cash. Spend it wisely. Cherish it. And above all, live it fully.

With gratitude and love,
Peggy

THE POWER OF NOW: UNLOCKING THE VALUE OF EACH DAY

THE POWER OF NOW: UNLOCKING
THE VALUE OF EACH DAY

Welcome to a journey of discovery, where we'll delve into the most valuable, yet often overlooked currency we possess—*time*. Our time on this beautiful blue planet is fleeting, each moment both a gift and an opportunity. Yet, it's so easy to forget this in the hustle and bustle of everyday life, where we're swept away by the current of tasks, to-dos, and deadlines.

In our quest to accumulate wealth, power, or knowledge, we frequently neglect to understand that every breath we take, every heartbeat we feel, is a testament to the most priceless asset in our possession. Each tick of the clock marks the passing of this relentless, yet profoundly precious commodity.

The Power of Now is not merely an introduction; it's an invitation to perceive time from a fresh perspective, to harness its immense potential, and to truly understand the wealth that lies in every passing moment. If you've ever found yourself saying, "I wish I had more time," this is your wake-up call. If you've ever wondered where the day, the week, the year went, this book is your *compass*. And if you've ever felt that time is controlling you rather than the other way around, this book is your path to liberation.

Today, we begin our journey. Today, we explore the depths of our most valuable asset. Today, we discover how to transform the fleeting currency of time into a wealth of experiences, growth, and fulfillment. Today, we embrace the power of now.

Because truly, isn't that all we ever have? Today.

"Your journey towards understanding and valuing your time starts here. Today. Now."

PART I

UNDERSTANDING THE VALUE OF TIME

CHAPTER 1

THE CURRENCY OF LIFE: TIME IS YOUR GREATEST ASSET

How often have you found yourself lamenting, "If only I had more time?" Time, dear reader, is the silent operator behind our lives, the hidden power that, when harnessed, can lead to extraordinary transformations.

Let's put this into perspective. If life were a market, time would be its most valuable currency. Unlike money, possessions, or even knowledge, time cannot be replenished once spent. Each second that passes becomes a part of history, forever beyond our reach. Time is relentless, never pausing, never waiting. It's the ultimate non-renewable resource.

Understanding this concept is the first step towards becoming the master of your moments, the architect of your days. Imagine your time as a vast reservoir. Each day, this reservoir is replenished with twenty-four hours—no more, no less. You can't save it for later, and you can't borrow from tomorrow. When the sun sets, the reservoir drains, regardless of how you choose to use your share.

The inherent value in each moment is staggering when we begin to view it through this lens. Each minute we spend mindlessly scrolling through social media, each hour lost to worrying about future uncertainties, each day gone by without purpose or joy—they all amount to a fortune in this precious currency, all gone.

Yet, every moment also holds a promise—the promise of choice. You can choose to let it slip away, unnoticed, and unvalued. Or you can seize it, shape it, and invest it in creating a life that truly resonates with your aspirations. The beauty of this choice lies in its simplicity and its power.

As we dive deeper into this journey, I want you to remember that every tick of the clock is an investment opportunity to learn, to grow, to love, to experience the myriad facets of life.

Consider this: if we reframe our perspective to see every morning as being gifted with a bag full of golden coins, each representing a minute in our day, how would we choose to spend them? Would we throw them around carelessly, or would we spend each one wisely, making sure it contributes to something meaningful?

This is the essence of the Today is Cash philosophy. From this point forward, I invite you to join me in embracing each moment as the unique, irreplaceable treasure it is. Because, my friend, time really is your greatest asset. Invest it wisely.

CHAPTER 2

YOUR DAILY BANK ACCOUNT: 24 HOURS DEPOSIT

If you think about it, every new dawn presents us with a unique kind of wealth: a fresh deposit of twenty-four hours in the bank of life, ready for us to withdraw and use. We're all millionaires in our own way, gifted with 1,440 minutes each day to spend as we please.

Think of it as your daily bank account, where time is the only currency. Just like money, time can be spent, wasted, or invested. However, unlike money, time, once spent, is gone forever. The clock keeps ticking, indifferent to our needs or desires.

Each of us, irrespective of our status, wealth, or power, receives the same daily deposit. From the most influential business mogul to the humblest of workers, we all get twenty-four hours. There's a sense of fairness in that, don't you think? What sets us apart, however, is how we choose to spend these hours.

This chapter is about making the most of your twenty-four-hour deposit. It's about recognizing the wealth of opportunities that each day brings and learning how to allocate your time to maximize its value.

First and foremost, we need to frame each day correctly. It's not just another rotation of the Earth; it's a valuable deposit into your account of existence. Understanding this is fundamental to changing our relationship with time.

Imagine waking up each morning and saying, "I have been gifted another twenty-four hours. How do I plan to invest them?" That tiny shift in perspective can make a world of difference.

Secondly, we should approach our time with the diligence of a wise investor. We wouldn't throw away our money without thought, would we? So why should we treat our time any differently? We need to be discerning, purposeful, and intentional with how we spend our minutes and hours.

So, let's stop looking at each day as just another tick on the calendar. Instead, let's consider it a unique opportunity, a precious deposit of twenty-four golden hours. Every sunrise brings a new wealth of time, and it's up to us to spend it wisely.

In the upcoming chapters, we'll explore how to manage your daily deposit effectively, identify common time wasters, and learn strategies for investing your time for the best returns.

Remember, every day you wake up, you're rich in the currency of time. The question is: how will you spend your wealth today?

CHAPTER 3

THE CLOCK IS TICKING: TIME IS UNFORGIVING

The hum of the universe is marked by the relentless ticking of time. Like a river, it flows uninterrupted, carving the canyons of our lives with each passing second. This constant, unyielding march of time is one of life's great certainties. And within this certainty, we find our most profound challenge and our greatest opportunity.

Time, my friends, is finite. Each of us has been allotted a set amount of time, a lease on life with an unknown expiration date. Yet, despite the inevitable ebbing away of our temporal existence, we often fall into the trap of assuming we have an infinite supply of days. The truth is every sunset brings us closer to our final dawn. This isn't intended to be morose but rather a stark reminder to acknowledge the value of each fleeting moment.

While the thought of time's finite nature may seem daunting, it's also incredibly liberating. It reinforces the need for mindful living, for being present in the here and now, instead of being lost in regrets of the past or anxieties about the future. Every tick of the clock is an invitation to engage fully with the present, to truly *live* each moment instead of merely existing.

Mindful living is like tuning in to the symphony of existence. It's about paying attention to the details —the warmth of the sun on your skin, the sound of laughter, the feeling of your heart beating within your chest. Each moment is rich with experiences just waiting to be noticed.

Being mindful of the ticking clock also encourages us to prioritize. When we become aware of the fleeting nature of time, we start to re-evaluate what truly deserves our hours and minutes. Consider the meetings that could have been emails, the hours spent mindlessly in front of screens, the time given to people or tasks that drain us rather than lift us. These timewasters become glaringly obvious.

In the face of an unforgiving clock, we learn to say no to the things that don't serve us, to the tasks that don't align with our values or goals. We become gatekeepers of our own time, fiercely protecting our daily deposit from being squandered.

This chapter serves as a reminder of time's finite, relentless nature, and the necessity of mindful living. As we progress through the pages ahead, we'll delve deeper into how we can make the most of the time we have, how we can tune in to the present, and how we can invest our hours wisely for a fulfilling, enriching life.

After all, the clock is ticking, and each second that passes is a second that will never come back. But within this transience lies the beautiful potential to live fully, intentionally, and meaningfully. Let's not waste a single moment.

PART II

USING, WASTING, OR INVESTING TIME

CHAPTER 4

SEIZE THE DAY: MAKING THE MOST OF NOW

We've laid the groundwork of understanding the precious nature of time and our daily deposit of twenty-four hours. We've discussed the power of mindful living and the ticking, unforgiving clock. Now, we turn our focus to action. This chapter is about seizing the day, about making the most of the present. It's about taking control of our time and becoming active participants in the unfolding story of our lives.

You see, time doesn't wait for us to decide. It doesn't pause for our indecision or our procrastination. It keeps moving, leaving us with a choice: we can let it slip through our fingers, or we can grab hold and make it count.

Harnessing the power of the present means acknowledging this choice. It means accepting that the present moment is the only moment where we can act, where we can effect change. The past is etched in stone, and the future is yet unwritten. The only time we have, the only time we can truly influence, is now.

So, how can we be proactive with our time? How can we make the most of our *now*? Here's some practical advice.

Prioritize	Not all tasks are created equal. Understand what truly matters to you and focus your energy there. Prioritize and separate your tasks into urgent, important, not urgent, and not important. This can provide clarity and help guide your decisions.
Break it Down	Large tasks can seem daunting, making us more likely to procrastinate. Break them down into smaller, manageable tasks. Small victories can fuel motivation and make the process less overwhelming. When writing this book, I decided to write for a period of time every day. This provided the opportunity to get the book written in a pre-determined period.

Eliminate Distractions	In our digital age, distractions are only a click away. Be aware of your time thieves: social media, unnecessary meetings, or even people who drain your time. Set boundaries and stick to them.
Schedule Me Time	This advice may seem counterintuitive, but scheduling time for rest and recreation can boost productivity and creativity. It's not wasted time; it's an investment in your mental well-being. Dr. Joseph Murphy was known to have said, "It is the quiet mind who gets things done."
Stay Flexible	Life is unpredictable. Keep some wiggle room in your schedule for unexpected events. Being too rigid can lead to stress and burnout.

Remember, every moment we spend is an investment. The return might not always be immediate or even tangible, but each moment invested in pursuing our passions, nurturing our relationships, and growing and learning brings us one step closer to a fulfilled, enriched life.

Seize your day, seize your moment, seize your now. This imperative is the essence of Today is Cash. The best time to make the most of your time is always, *always* now.

CHAPTER 5

THE TIME SINK: HOW WE WASTE OUR MOST PRECIOUS RESOURCE

Despite the value we've placed on time, there's no denying that we're all guilty of squandering it at some point. This isn't a judgment, just an acknowledgment of our human tendency to let precious moments slip away into the void of nonproductivity. This chapter is about shining a light on these time sinks and understanding how we can navigate around them.

Let's consider some common timewasters.

Digital devices One major culprit is undoubtedly our **digital devices**: a quick check of email, a brief scroll on social media, a short video on YouTube. These seemingly harmless activities can quickly spiral into hours of wasted time. The internet is like a maze; it's easy to get lost and harder to find your way out.

Endless meetings	Then there are the **endless meetings**: discussions that could have been handled with emails, brainstorming sessions without a clear agenda. While collaboration is crucial, inefficient meetings can drain our most precious resource.
Procrastination	And let's not forget about **procrastination**, the thief of time that promises us that we can always do it later. It lures us with the comfort of delay, only to leave us in the whirlwind of rushed deadlines and unfulfilled tasks.

To illustrate, let's delve into some real-life examples of timewasters.

Consider Sally, a personal coach who was feeling overwhelmed with the marketing of her business. Upon reflection, she realized that she was spending at least two hours a day on her phone during work hours, checking social media and shopping online.

Or take Billy, a small business owner, who found that his team was spending an average of fifteen hours per week in meetings. After implementing a more streamlined meeting structure, ensuring that each meeting had a written agenda, and reducing the time spent in unnecessary discussions, productivity soared.

In each of these examples, time was being wasted, but once the time culprits were identified, the individuals could take steps to address the problem. Sally better managed the digital distractions, Billy trimmed the bloated meetings and implemented a more mindful, efficient use of time.

We all have our own versions of Sally's phone habit or Billy's endless meetings. The key is to *identify* them and *actively work* towards minimizing their drain on your time. Remember, time management is not about achieving perfection but about making consistent improvements.

In the following chapters, we'll explore strategies for turning these time sinks into time wells—sources of productivity and satisfaction. *But the first step is recognizing where our time is currently leaking.*

Because the truth is, time, like water, will always find a way to slip away. It's up to us to ensure it's not trickling down the drain of unproductive activities but flowing into the river of meaningful experiences and accomplishments. After all, we're the masters of our time, and it's high time we acted like it.

CHAPTER 6

THE COMPOUND EFFECT: INVESTING TIME WISELY

As we've explored, time is our most precious asset. It's the currency of life, and how we choose to spend it shapes the quality of our experiences and, ultimately, our lives. The good news is that when we invest time wisely, the returns are exponential. This is the power of the *compound effect*, and it's our focus in this chapter.

Imagine if you decided to learn a new word each day. It's a small investment, taking only a couple of minutes. But over a year, you would have added 365 new words to your vocabulary. Over five years, that's 1,825 words! This is the compound effect in action—*small, consistent investments of time leading to significant outcomes.*

Now, let's apply this concept to the broader spectrum of our lives, from personal growth and relationships to our careers and passions. The compounding nature of these investments can create a ripple effect of positivity, contributing to our overall well-being and fulfillment.

Personal Growth Investing in your personal growth can take many forms. It might be learning a new skill, nurturing a hobby, or working on personal attributes like resilience or empathy. Whatever form it takes, remember that *consistency is key*. Even a few minutes a day can lead to substantial growth over time.

Relationships Relationships need time to flourish. Consistent, quality time invested in your relationships—be it family, friends, or your significant other—can deepen bonds and enrich your life. Remember, it's not about grand gestures; often, it's the small, everyday moments of connection that matter most.

Career Whether learning a new aspect of your job, networking, or brainstorming innovative ideas, investing time in your career can have long-lasting impacts. The skills you learn, the relationships you build, and the problems you solve can open doors and create opportunities for advancement.

Passions	Investing time in what you love is an investment in your happiness. Whether it's painting, hiking, reading, or anything that sparks joy, giving time to your passions can provide a sense of fulfillment, reduce stress, and boost your overall mood.
Health	A few minutes of daily exercise, mindful eating, and regular health check-ups are all investments in your health. And remember, health isn't just physical. Investing time in mental health, like mindfulness practices or journaling, can greatly enhance your quality of life.

It's crucial to remember that the compound effect works both ways. Just as *positive actions* can accumulate into significant results, so too can *negative actions* lead to detrimental outcomes. Thus, being mindful of where your time is invested is just as important as investing itself.

So, here's my challenge. Identify one area of your life where you'd like to see growth. Start with small, manageable time investments. Remember, it's not about making massive changes overnight but about consistent, daily effort. And watch, as the compound effect takes hold over time, and these small investments lead to big, beautiful results.

Because in the grand scheme of things, our time isn't just our currency; it's our legacy. Let's invest it wisely.

PART III

TOOLS AND STRATEGIES FOR TIME MANAGEMENT

CHAPTER 7

BUILDING YOUR TIME PORTFOLIO: DIVERSIFYING YOUR DAY

You've probably heard the term *portfolio* in relation to finances. It's a diverse mix of investments designed to balance risk and return. However, this concept isn't exclusive to finance; it can also be applied to our most valuable asset—time. So, let's discuss how we can create a balanced time portfolio and diversify our days.

The concept of diversifying your day is all about balance. Picture your day as a pie chart. Each slice represents an activity, be it work, family time, personal development, leisure, or health. Now, if the slices are disproportionately large or small, the pie as a whole feels off-balance.

The idea here is to create a balanced portfolio of activities— one that meets our needs, fuels our passions, maintains our health, nurtures our relationships, and fulfills our responsibilities. It's not about every slice being equal in size, but about *each one being proportionate to its importance in our life.*

So, how do we go about building a well-diversified time portfolio? Follow these steps.

Understand Your Priorities	The first step is to understand what's most important to you: your work, your relationships, your personal growth, your passions, your health. Rank these in order of importance. This isn't about creating a rigid hierarchy, but about gaining clarity on what matters most to you.
Allocate Your Time	Now, think about how you can distribute your time across these areas. Aim for balance, but remember, balance doesn't always mean equal. You may need to spend more time on work during the week, but you can balance it out with quality family time on the weekend.
Regularly Review Your Portfolio	Regularly review and adjust your portfolio. Just like a financial portfolio, your time portfolio may need rebalancing from time to time.

Be Flexible	It's important to remain adaptable. Life is unpredictable, and sticking too rigidly to your planned portfolio can lead to stress. Be prepared to make changes when necessary.
Remember to Recharge	Last, but by no means least, don't forget to allocate time for rest. No matter how balanced your portfolio, without time to recharge, burnout is inevitable.

As we journey through life, our time portfolio will change. Different stages will call for different allocations. The key is to stay *aware*, *flexible*, and *focused* on maintaining a balance that serves our current needs and long-term goals.

In the end, diversifying your day is all about embracing the full spectrum of human experience. It's about understanding that our time is best spent when it's spread across a range of activities that reflect the richness and diversity of our lives. After all, life isn't meant to be a single-note melody; it's a symphony, with each section playing its part in creating a beautiful whole.

CHAPTER 8

THE TIME BUDGET: PLANNING YOUR DAY LIKE YOUR FINANCES

When it comes to finances, we all understand the concept of *budgeting*. We keep track of our income and expenses, ensuring that we live within our means and save for the future. But what if I told you that the same principles that apply to budgeting money can also be applied to budgeting time? Welcome to the concept of time budgeting.

Just as financial budgeting is all about allocating your monetary resources to meet your financial goals, *time budgeting is about allocating your hours to align with your personal and professional goals.* Let's delve into this concept a bit more, and I'll share some time management techniques and tools to help you master your time budget.

Identify Your Time Income	First, identify your time income. In this context, your income is the amount of time available to you in a day—twenty-four hours.
List Your Time Expenses	Your time expenses are the activities that consume your time. This includes everything from work, family time, exercise, leisure activities, sleep, and anything else you spend your time on.
Create Your Time Budget	With your income and expenses in mind, create a time budget. Allocate specific hours to each activity based on its importance. Be realistic, keeping in mind that the sum of your allocations should not exceed your income (twenty-four hours).
Track Your Time	Just as you track your financial spending, track your time spending too. There are many time-tracking apps available, or you could simply use a diary or spreadsheet. The aim is to have a clear picture of where your time goes.
Review and Adjust	Regularly review your time budget. If you find that you're consistently overspending time in one area and underspending in another, it's time to readjust.

Let's look at an example. Suppose Betty, a freelance copy-writer, has been feeling overwhelmed and unproductive. She decides to implement time budgeting. After tracking her time for a week, she realizes she's spending too much time on administrative tasks and not enough on her actual creative work or personal development.

Using this insight, she revises her time budget, allocating specific blocks for administrative tasks, creative work, skill development, and relaxation. Over time, she finds that she's more productive, less stressed, and has more time for personal growth and leisure.

One tool Betty might use is the Pomodoro Technique. This involves working for a set amount of time (say, twenty-five minutes), then taking a short break (say, five minutes). This is known as one *Pomodoro*. After four Pomodoros, she would take a longer break. This can be a helpful way to manage time and maintain focus during work hours.

Remember, time is a resource just as money is. And, just like money, *if you don't control how you spend time, it will control you*. By taking charge of your time through budgeting, you can ensure that you're investing it in the activities that truly matter to you.

In the end, mastering your time is about more than just productivity and efficiency. It's about creating a life that reflects your values and aspirations. So, take charge of your time, and watch as your life transforms in ways you could have only imagined. After all, your time is your life. Budget it wisely.

CHAPTER 9

THE TIME AUDIT: EVALUATING YOUR TIME EXPENDITURE

Have you ever found yourself at the end of a day wondering where all your time went? Have you ever felt like you've been busy all day but can't seem to pinpoint what you've achieved? Well, you're not alone. This is where a time audit comes into play.

A time audit is a method to evaluate how you're actually spending your time, as opposed to how you think you're spending it. The goal is to identify where your time is going, so you can adjust and align your activities with your goals and priorities. It's like taking your car in for a check-up, but this time, the mechanic is you, and the car is your daily schedule.

So, how do you conduct a time audit? It's simpler than you might think.

Track Your Time	For at least one week, record how you spend your time. Write down every activity, no matter how small, and how long it takes. Be honest with yourself—this is about accuracy, not judgment.
Categorize Your Activities	Once you've tracked your time, categorize your activities. Common categories might include work, family time, leisure, sleep, exercise, personal growth, chores, and so on.
Evaluate Your Findings	Review your records and ask yourself some key questions. Are you spending time on what matters most to you? Are there activities consuming more time than they should? Are there activities you wish you had more time for?
Make Adjustments	Based on your findings, make adjustments to your schedule. You may find you need to delegate certain tasks, eliminate timewasters, or simply make more intentional choices about how you spend your time.

Let's look at a real-life example. Meet John, a small business owner. Despite working long hours, he always felt behind and stressed. He decided to conduct a time audit. After tracking his time for a week, he found he was spending a lot of time responding to emails, which left little time for strategic planning.

Upon realizing this, John decided to limit checking and responding to emails to specific time blocks twice a day. This freed up several hours each week, which he could then invest in strategic planning and growing his business. This small change made a huge difference in his productivity and stress levels.

That's the beauty of a time audit. It's a reality check that shows us where our time is actually going, providing us the insights we need to make meaningful changes. A time audit is not about squeezing more tasks into your day. It's about making sure your time—your life—is being spent in a way that aligns with your values, your goals, and your happiness.

Remember, conducting a time audit is not a one-time activity. As our lives evolve, so do our schedules. Regular time audits can help ensure we're continually aligning our time expenditure with our evolving goals and priorities.

So, are you ready to take the driver's seat and steer your time in the direction you truly want to go? Conduct a time audit and be the master of your time, and ultimately, your life.

CHAPTER 10

CULTIVATING PROSPERITY: THE POWER OF THOUGHT AND FEELING

There is an undeniable force within us all, a kind of magnetic power that draws experiences into our lives based on the quality of our thoughts and feelings. This is not some mystical, esoteric concept, but a fundamental principle that underlies our reality. Our thoughts and feelings can shape our lives, including our level of wealth and prosperity.

To understand this, think about a time when you were in a great mood. Everything seemed to go your way, didn't it? Conversely, during periods of gloom and despair, it's as if the universe conspires to bring you more of the same. This isn't just coincidence; it's the *law of attraction* at work.

Feeling prosperous, feeling rich, can be instrumental in actually attracting wealth and abundance into your life. The power of positive thinking is more than a motivational mantra; it's a mindset that can shift your reality. Our thoughts and feelings are like seeds, and when we sow seeds of abundance, we cultivate a garden of prosperity.

Now, cultivating feelings of prosperity doesn't mean ignoring reality or denying the existence of problems. It means choosing to focus your energy on *opportunities* rather than obstacles, *solutions* rather than problems. It's about creating a mental state that is conducive to growth and progress.

So, how do we nurture these feelings of prosperity? Here are some suggestions.

Awareness   The first step is awareness. Pay attention to your thoughts. Are they generally positive, or do they often drift towards the negative? Do you visualize yourself achieving success and wealth, or do you worry about lack and scarcity? *Recognizing your dominant thought patterns* is the first step towards changing them.

Mindfulness   Next, practice mindfulness. When a negative thought or feeling arises, don't suppress it, or pretend it's not there. Acknowledge it, and then consciously choose to let it go and replace it with a positive one. This isn't easy, and it requires practice, but the effects can be life changing.

Daily Affirmations
Finally, engage in daily affirmations. Affirmations are positive statements that can help you overcome self-sabotaging thoughts. Every morning, tell yourself, "I am prosperous. I am attracting wealth and abundance." Repeat it until you *truly* believe it. The more you say it, the more your mind will accept it as a reality, and the more your life will reflect it.

Cultivating feelings of prosperity can be a powerful tool for wealth creation. Remember: Today is Cash. Treat each day as an opportunity to grow, to succeed, and to attract wealth. Make the conscious choice to feel rich and watch as the universe reciprocates.

Remember, your thoughts and feelings are powerful instruments, and when properly attuned, they can attract boundless prosperity into your life. This is another key investment in your life's wealth, in the bank of life. Invest wisely.

CHAPTER 11

A WEALTH OF GRATITUDE: ATTRACTING ABUNDANCE THROUGH APPRECIATION

As we navigate our journey towards understanding and harnessing the essence of Today is Cash, we must also discuss a fundamental and transformative tool: gratitude. Gratitude, the simple act of expressing thankfulness and appreciation for the good in our lives, can significantly influence our experiences, perceptions, and the outcomes of our days.

Gratitude isn't just an emotion; it's a daily practice that can shift our mindset and open our hearts to the abundance that life has to offer. It's akin to the seeds of prosperity we discussed in the previous chapter: the more seeds of gratitude we sow, the more our garden of prosperity grows.

Gratitude is the thread that weaves together all aspects of our lives into a rich tapestry of abundance. It makes us aware of the wealth that already exists in our lives: the wealth of relationships, experiences, opportunities, and even challenges that make us who we are. By recognizing and appreciating this wealth, we not only enjoy our current circumstances more but also attract even more abundance into our lives.

So, how can we cultivate a daily practice of gratitude? Try these suggestions.

Gratitude Journal	Each morning or night, write down three things for which you are grateful. These don't have to be big, life-changing events; they can be as simple as a warm cup of coffee or a smile from a stranger. By noting these moments of joy, we start to focus more on the positive aspects of our lives.
Gratitude to Others	Make it a habit to thank the people in your life. Thank your spouse for their support, your co-workers for their hard work, or your friends for their companionship. Verbalizing your appreciation not only makes others feel valued but also reinforces your sense of gratitude.

Mindful Moments	Take a few minutes each day to sit quietly and reflect on the things for which you are grateful. This mindfulness practice can help you stay grounded and focused on the positive aspects of your life, even amid chaos or stress.
Gratitude Reminders	Set reminders on your phone or leave sticky notes around your house to remind you to pause and appreciate the moment. These small prompts can help you maintain a gratitude mindset throughout your day.
Gratitude in Challenges	This may be the toughest one, but it's also the most rewarding. Try to find something to be grateful for even in challenging situations. This doesn't mean ignoring your problems, but it does mean recognizing that every challenge is an opportunity for growth and learning.

Cultivating a daily practice of gratitude is like making a daily deposit in the bank of life. And the returns on this investment are incredible: a more positive outlook, greater happiness, and an abundance of wealth in all aspects of life.

By appreciating each *today* as the cash it truly is, you can attract even more good into your life and, ultimately, live a life rich in happiness, fulfillment, and prosperity. Remember: Today is Cash. Make every day count by embracing gratitude.

CHAPTER 12

STARTING LINE: BUILDING WEALTH FROM WHERE YOU ARE

I n our exploration of the mantra, "Today is Cash," we've covered a myriad of principles and tools to help you redefine and build wealth. However, you might be wondering, "But what if I'm starting from scratch? What if I'm not just at ground zero, but in the negatives?" Don't fret. I assure you, it's never too late to start, and your past circumstances do not dictate your future wealth.

This belief isn't just theory; it's a lesson I've learned firsthand. Like many, I wasn't born with a silver spoon in my mouth. My early years were marked by scarcity and financial instability. I spent my young adulthood entrapped in the vicious cycle of debt, barely keeping my head above water. However, it was through this very struggle that I learned the most critical wealth-building principle: *your financial past does not determine your financial future.*

Regardless of your starting point, you can choose to take control of your financial destiny today. Here are some insights that helped me turn my financial life around.

Reframe Your Mindset	If you believe you can't achieve wealth because of your past, you've already lost half the battle. The first step towards wealth creation is developing a growth mindset and believing in your capacity to change your financial situation.
Education is Key	Financial literacy is crucial in this journey. Educate yourself about managing money, investing, and creating passive income streams. Information is power, and there's no better time than now, in this era of readily available online resources, to empower yourself.
Build a Budget	Knowing where your money goes is critical. Create a budget that reflects your current financial reality, helps you manage your debts, and allows you to save and invest.

Invest in Yourself   Investing isn't just about putting your money into stocks, bonds, or real estate. It's also about investing in yourself—your education, skills, and personal growth. The returns on this kind of investment are priceless.

Slow and Steady Wins the Race   Wealth creation isn't a sprint; it's a marathon. It's not about quick, risky ventures but about consistent, disciplined investment of time and resources.

Embrace Failure   Mistakes are inevitable. However, every failure is an opportunity to learn and grow. Don't let fear of failure stop you from taking calculated risks necessary for wealth creation.

Be Patient   It takes time to turn around a difficult financial situation. Be patient with yourself. Celebrate small victories, keep learning from your mistakes, and continue investing in your future.

I want you to know that no matter where you are starting from, wealth is possible for you. You have within you all the resources you need to transform your financial future. Your past may have shaped you, but it doesn't define you.

Remember: Today is Cash. You have the power to make today the first day of your journey towards wealth and prosperity.

CHAPTER 13

CULTIVATING PROSPERITY: MAKING WEALTH A HABIT

We are, all of us, creatures of habit. Our habits shape our actions, which, in turn, shape our destinies. If you look closely, you'll find that the financial situation you are in today is largely the result of your past habits. To quote the famous saying, "The secret of your future is hidden in your daily routine." If you wish to cultivate prosperity, you need to make wealth a habit.

However, what does it mean *to make wealth a habit*? It's not about obsessively focusing on money or getting stuck in the rat race. Instead, it's about incorporating daily practices that foster a prosperity mindset, creating a fertile ground for wealth to grow. It's about ensuring that every action you take aligns with the mantra, "Today is Cash."

Let me guide you through the process of making wealth a habit.

Mindset Matters	Begin your day by setting a positive tone for your thoughts. Morning affirmations are a great tool to gear your mind towards prosperity. Recite affirmations like, "I am a magnet for wealth" or "I am financially free and prosperous."
Practice Gratitude	Every day, express gratitude for what you already have. It's a powerful way to cultivate a prosperity mindset, as it keeps your focus on abundance rather than lack.
Set Clear Financial Goals	Be clear about what you want your financial future to look like. Break down your long-term goals into short-term achievable targets. Remember: *what gets measured, gets managed.*
Educate Yourself	Make it a daily habit to learn something new about money management, investing, or wealth creation. Knowledge is your greatest asset.
Save and Invest Consistently	The most effective way to accumulate wealth is to save and invest regularly, no matter how small the amount. Remember, consistency is key.

Visualize Success	Regularly visualize your financial goals as if they've already been achieved. This practice aligns your subconscious mind with your financial goals and accelerates the manifestation process.
Take Inspired Action	Every day, take at least one action that moves you closer to your financial goals. It can be as simple as reading a chapter from a finance book, tracking your expenses, or researching investment options.

Cultivating prosperity is not a one-time event but a daily practice. You might not see the results overnight, but remember, small, consistent steps can lead to big results. Your daily habits sow the seeds for your future prosperity. In time, these seeds will grow into a tree of wealth, providing shade and fruit for you and generations to come.

Remember: Today is Cash. Today is the perfect day to start cultivating the habit of prosperity.

CHAPTER 14

THE CYCLE OF PROSPERITY: THE POWER OF GIVING

Have you ever noticed how nature works in cycles? The water that evaporates from the oceans eventually falls back to the earth as rain, nourishing the land and replenishing the oceans. It's a never-ending cycle of *giving* and *receiving*. This concept is not only central to the natural world but also to the world of wealth and prosperity. This chapter is about that concept: the power of giving.

It's easy to fall into the trap of believing that wealth accumulation is a one-way street, that the end goal is to hoard as much as you can for yourself. But true prosperity isn't about hoarding; it's about flow. *Money is a form of energy, and just like any other form of energy, it needs to keep moving to maintain its vitality.*

But here's the catch. Many of us hold on to a scarcity mindset. We hold tightly to what we have, fearing that giving will leave us with less. However, the universe operates on a different principle. *The more you give, the more you receive.* It's a universal law as real and dependable as gravity.

That's not to say that you should give with the expectation of receiving. The most rewarding form of giving is unconditional, done out of love, compassion, and a genuine desire to make a difference. The rewards you reap are not always material. They come in the form of joy, fulfillment, and a sense of purpose that no amount of money can buy.

Now, you might be thinking, "I don't have much. What can I possibly give?" But giving isn't just about money. It's about sharing whatever resources you have, whether that's time, skills, knowledge, or even a listening ear. You might not realize it, but even these seemingly small acts of kindness can make a significant impact on someone else's life.

In the grand scheme of things, practicing generosity serves a dual purpose. It not only enriches the lives of those around you but also nurtures your own prosperity mindset. It's a reminder that wealth is not a limited resource, that there's enough for everyone. By freely giving, you're sending a message to the universe that you live in abundance, not scarcity.

So, as you go about your journey to financial prosperity, *remember the power of giving*. Understand that you are a part of a bigger cycle of prosperity, a cycle that's as much about giving as it is about receiving. It's not just about becoming rich in wealth; it's about becoming rich in spirit, in compassion, and in generosity. That's the true essence of the mantra, "Today is Cash."

TIME RICH: BUILDING WEALTH IN THE BANK OF LIFE

As we reach the end of our journey together, I want to congratulate you. By reading this far, you've already demonstrated your commitment to mastering your time. You've taken the first steps towards becoming time rich—a wealth that transcends monetary measures.

Throughout this book, we've reframed time as our most valuable asset, comparable to a daily deposit of twenty-four hours in the bank of life. We've talked about understanding the value of each second, minute, and hour, and about recognizing the brutal truth: *time, once spent, is irrecoverable.*

We've delved into the ways we can use, waste, or invest our time, and learned that our day-to-day choices shape the quality of our lives. We discovered that seizing the day, avoiding time sinks, and investing time wisely could set the stage for profound personal growth and satisfaction.

Together, we've examined tools and strategies for time management, likening them to financial planning concepts.

From diversifying your day, like a balanced portfolio, to treating your schedule as a budget and auditing your time expenditure, we've equipped ourselves with a toolkit to effectively manage our time.

Now, as we stand at the precipice of newfound knowledge and insights, the next steps are yours to take. *The power to transform your relationship with time rests in your hands.*

Becoming time-rich isn't about cramming more tasks into each day. It's about living in alignment with your values, your passions, your goals. It's about investing your time in ways that fill your life with joy, meaning, and purpose. It's about realizing that today, this moment, is the greatest asset you own.

So, as you move forward, remember: Today is Cash. Don't let it slip through your fingers unattended. Invest it wisely. Cherish it. And make every second count.

Your journey to becoming *time rich* starts now. It's time to step into the world with a newfound respect for each ticking second. It's time to start building wealth in the grandest bank of all—the bank of life.

Remember, the future is born from what you do today. So, make today count. After all, today is all we have. *Today truly is cash.* And, my dear reader, it's time for you to cash in.

ABOUT THE AUTHOR

Peggy McColl has dedicated her life to making a positive difference in the lives of hundreds of millions of people around the world, from her immediate family to cherished readers like you. She is a world-renowned wealth, business, and manifestation expert as well as the New York Times Best Selling Author of *Your Destiny Switch: Master Your Key Emotions And Attract the Life of Your Dreams.*

Throughout her career, Peggy has been coined "Your Destiny Maker" and "The Prosperity Mentor". She has worked with – and been endorsed by – other icons in the personal development field, from Bob Proctor and Neale Donald Walsch to Mark Victor Hansen and Marianne Williamson.

Peggy's books, events and online programs inspire and instruct people to heal their past, reach their maximum potential, take massive quantum leaps, and truly create their own destiny by design through simple, step-by-step self-realization.

To explore more ways Peggy can help you reach your goals and live your dreams, please visit:

http://PeggyMcColl.com

TRANSFORM YOUR LIFE WITH "THE CASH OF TODAY: MASTERING TIME FOR PROSPERITY" PROGRAM

Dear Reader,

If you've been moved and inspired by "Today is Cash", you're probably eager to start applying the principles you've learned to your own life. But where do you start? And how do you ensure you're truly maximizing each day to its fullest potential?

I'm thrilled to offer you an exclusive opportunity to dive even deeper into the life-changing principles in "Today is Cash". Introducing "The Cash of Today: Mastering Time for Prosperity" program, a comprehensive, step-by-step course designed to help you understand, implement, and master the concept of time as your greatest asset.

In this transformative program, you'll not only learn how to value your time but also discover the tools and strategies necessary for effective time management. From understanding the nature of time to using it wisely and investing it for maximum yield, we leave no stone unturned.

Here's what you can expect from The Cash of Today: Mastering Time for Prosperity program:

- In-depth Lessons: We dive deep into the principles outlined in "Today is Cash", providing you with comprehensive knowledge and understanding.

- Practical Exercises: Each module comes with actionable tasks and exercises, turning your newfound knowledge into practical, everyday habits.

- Tools and Strategies: We equip you with effective tools and proven strategies to help you manage your time, become more productive, and attract wealth into your life.

- A Supportive Community: Join a like-minded community, where you can share experiences, learn from others, and build lifelong relationships.

Whether you're a busy entrepreneur, an aspiring individual, or someone who wants to create more value in your life, this program is designed to transform the way you view and use your time.

Don't let another second go by without making it count!

Visit http://PeggyMcColl.com to learn more about The Cash of Today: Mastering Time for Prosperity program and take the first step towards a more abundant, time-rich life.

Your Time is Cash. Make it Count.

Giving a Voice to Creativity!

With every donation, a voice will be given to the creativity that lies within the hearts of our children living with diverse challenges.

By making this difference, children that may not have been given the opportunity to have their Heart Heard will have the freedom to create beautiful works of art and musical creations.

Donate by visiting

HeartstobeHeard.com

We thank you.

Made in the USA
Monee, IL
21 August 2023

41420075R00069